The Tiger Cubs & the Chimp

The True Story of How Anjana the Chimp Helped Raise Two Baby Tigers

Bhagavan "Doc" ANTLE with Thea FELDMAN
Photographs by Barry BLAND

Henry Holt and Company • New York

Henry Holt and Company, LLC
Publishers since 1866
175 Fifth Avenue
New York, New York 10010
mackids.com

Library of Congress Cataloging-in-Publication Data
Antle, Bhagavan.
The tiger cubs and the chimp : the true story of how Anjana the chimp helped raise two
baby tigers / Bhagavan "Doc" Antle with Thea Feldman ; photographs by Barry Bland.
pages   cm
ISBN 978-0-8050-9319-3 (hardcover)
1. Tiger cubs—Juvenile literature. 2. Chimpanzees—Behavior—Juvenile literature.
I. Feldman, Thea. II. Title.
QL737.C23A58 2013   599.885—dc23   2012047320

First Edition—2013 / Designed by Véronique Lefèvre Sweet

Printed in China by South China Printing Co. Ltd., Dongguan City,
Guangdong Province

1 3 5 7 9 10 8 6 4 2

*To all the men and women who have
dedicated their lives to wildlife preservation*
—B. A.

Chuff! Chuff!
Mitra and Shiva are saying hello to you.
Can you say hello to them?

Mitra and Shiva are twin brothers.
They live on an animal preserve.

What do Mitra and Shiva do
at the preserve?

They run.
They play.

They like to
swim, too.

At the preserve,
there are things to sniff
and logs to scratch.

Their favorite toy is a ball.

Most tigers have orange and black fur.

Mitra and Shiva are different.
Their fur is white and black.

Most tigers have yellow eyes.

Mitra's and Shiva's eyes are blue.

Something else is different
about them, too.

Mitra and Shiva were raised
by a human named China
and a chimpanzee named Anjana.
China takes care of animal babies
who need help.
Anjana was one of those babies.
Now Anjana helps China.
Anjana takes care of animal babies, too.

Why did Mitra and Shiva need help?
When they were three days old,
there was a big storm at the preserve.
The tiny cubs were in danger
and their mother couldn't help.
They needed a person
to keep them safe.
China was that person.
And Anjana was her special helper!

China fed the cubs warm milk.
Anjana fed them, too.
How did Anjana know what to do?
She watched China.
She did what China did.

China carried the cubs a lot.
Anjana carried them, too.
She carried one cub at a time
to China.
"Thank you, Anjana," said China.
"You are a good helper."

Sometimes Mitra and Shiva got scared.
When that happened,
Anjana put one arm around each cub.
"*Boop, boop, boop,*" she said.
That meant, "I am here with you.
You are okay."

The cubs crawled all over Anjana.
Anjana made a noise that sounded like
"*Ha, ha, ha!*"
That meant, "I am happy."

One of Anjana's friends
at the preserve
was Suryia, an orangutan.
Sometimes Suryia liked to play
with Mitra and Shiva, too.

Mitra and Shiva grew and grew.
They grew big and strong.
Now they live with other tigers
at the preserve.

Sometimes they still see
Anjana and China.

Sometimes they still see
Anjana and China.

Mitra and Shiva are happy
and healthy.
Roar!
That means,
"Thank you, Anjana!"

Author's Note

Anjana the chimpanzee lives at a wildlife preserve in Myrtle Beach, South Carolina, called T.I.G.E.R.S. (The Institute for Greatly Endangered and Rare Species). Although many different interspecies friendships have been documented, it is rare to find the relationship that bonds Anjana with Mitra and Shiva.

How did it happen? At the T.I.G.E.R.S. preserve, animals enjoy a nurtured, fulfilled life. Anjana is less concerned with survival because her needs and security are met with love and care. This allows her intellect and curiosity to grow. Encouraged by seeing other animals interacting with their human caretakers, Anjana overcame her natural aversion to species such as tigers in this comfortable environment.

Bhagavan "Doc" Antle founded the T.I.G.E.R.S. preserve to provide grassroots support and protection for endangered species. For nearly thirty years, T.I.G.E.R.S. and its parent organization, the Rare Species Fund, have provided funding, training, and staff to wildlife initiatives worldwide. For more information, visit RareSpeciesFund.org.